*View from South Queensferry before the Forth Rail Bridge began —
showing in the distance, the Castle and Rock of Inchgarvie.*

The raft used for survey of foundations

*One of the towers as it appeared in 1887 showing the
cantilever arms beginning to reach out on either side.*

A close up of the bridge today showing the Castle and Rock of Inchgarvie "the keystone of the bridge" and two of the piers four of which support each of the three towers.

Floating out a caisson from the South Queensferry shore.

*Granite blocks being constructed within a caisson,
forming one of the piers*

BRIDGES, ISLANDS
AND
VILLAGES
OF THE
FIRTH OF FORTH

by Malcolm Archibald

Introduction

Where is the haunted castle with a hidden treasure? Why did the king maroon a dumb nurse and two orphans on an island in the Forth? How did a Fifer who operated as a buccaneer in the South Seas become world famous? Who was executed for whipping up a storm off the coast? What are the grim secrets of the Bass Rock and why was it a place of terror? When did a Spanish Armada ship call at Anstruther?

These are just a few of the questions answered during this enthralling journey around the Forth coast.

Malcolm Archibald tells the fascinating stories of towns and villages; islands and bridges. Along the way we meet all sorts of colourful characters including smugglers, highwaymen, heroes, kings, ghosts and witches.

Discover the dramatic Bannockburn story behind a church stone at Crail, the truth about a lighthouse keeper and his family wiped out in a tragedy, the Cockenzie folk who caught whales to feed their hungry children, and how Portobello came into being because a seaman had his ear cut off.

Why was there cannon fire and bitter fighting on Leith Links? Who were the combatants in the oyster wars, what kind of big money was at stake, and who won? Why did treasure hunters pillage Inchcolm? How many men did it take to build the Forth Rail Bridge, how many died in the process, and how much paint is needed to keep it from rusting away? What was it like using the Forth ferries, how many were there, and how did the Road Bridge dream become a reality? Why is there a link between Robert Louis Stevenson's "Treasure Island" and a North Berwick inn? How did clansmen show total loyalty in the face of terrible butchery at the Battle of Inverkeithing? What dreadful trickery did monks perform off Aberdour beach with a knight's body in a lead coffin? How did a king's death at Kinghorn spark a war that lasted 100 years? Who told his killer with his dying breath, "You've spoilt a better face than your own"? How did gentle prophet John Muir and wild warrior Black Agnes put Dunbar on the map?

For all the answers and the key to many other strange secrets of the Forth coast read on!

"Bridges, Islands and Villages of the Firth of Forth" was published by Lang Syne Publishers Ltd, Old School, Blanefield, Glasgow, in 1990 and was printed by Waterside Printers at the same address.
Copyright Lang Syne Publishers Ltd 1990.
ISBN 185217 141 3.

Preface

This is not a guide to the Forth, but an introduction. The Firth of Forth is, and has been for centuries, one of the major gateways to Scotland. The Firth contains Scotland's capital and her main historical ports, some of the most significant islands in her past and a handful of her battlefields. The Firth is a major fishing area, a major trading area and has been a major invasion area.

Romans, Vikings, English, French, Spanish and Dutch have sailed here, Germans have flown overhead. All have contributed something — as have the odd American and even a Forth born Russian Admiral. The American was John Paul Jones, who crept in to attack Leith but was beset by contrary winds. For a while he put the Forth in a panic, guns were dragged from Edinburgh Castle to repel him, muskets shaken out and even a minister of Kirkcaldy used to pray for a gale.

The prayers worked and Paul Jones was driven out without a shot being fired.

The Forth is full of tales like that, each village has its quota, each beach its ballad, each headland its story.

In this book the reader is led from the southern entrance, the Bass Rock and North Berwick, westward to the two Bridges, across to Fife and eastward to the Island of May. A lot has been missed out.

Nothing has been said of the Forth upstream of the Bridges for that deserves a book of its own. To try and include Blackness and Bo'ness, Grangemouth and Stirling, Kincardine and atmospheric Culross, Limekilns and Rosyth would have been impossible. St Margaret's Hope, where Saint Margaret landed on her way to a nunnery, ending up as a queen, has a story of its own.

Even in the section covered there is cruelty. Burntisland has a long and honourable history, Kirkcaldy and Dysart as much or more. The two Wemysses, Methil and the fishing villages between Earlsferry and Pittenweem deserve more than a mention, as do Aberlady, for its bay, and Prestonpans for its battle.

And then there's Musselburgh — and Granton.

However, this book is intended to give an idea of the atmosphere, of the character of the Forth. And there is far too much character for it to be lost.

Stormy days on the Bass Rock!

Stark sentinel of the Forth, the Bass hoists three and a half hundred feet of guano streaked rock to glower down the passage of Scottish history.

A place of awesome impregnability, it would seem a strange home for a holy man yet at least one saint settled amidst the plunging gannets to study the scriptures as North Sea rollers smashed to his psalms. Saint Baldred of the Bass; the name carries conviction, a sense of rightness which has left memories among the Lothian place names. Baldred's cell was on a terrace on the south and he seems to have lived in harmony with his surroundings.

In time his cell mouldered and a chapel took its place — the Church of the parish of the Bass. Surely, at seven acres, the smallest parish in Scotland. But maybe it was needed to pacify the wild men who were about to make the rock their own. The Bass was to put its sanctimonious past behind it and embark on a long period of violence and repression.

As the Dark Ages flared into glittering mediaevalism, Norman war-lords grasped gustily at half-formed kingdoms. Scotland became the target for English kings. Mailed armies marched and St George's blood red cross fluttered in the Forth; Dunbar Castle was invested and Black Agnes, Countess of March, dusted her defences as her arrows held the English at bay. Offshore, a mercenary fleet prevented supplies from reaching her and Dunbar was in danger of defeat.

There is always a way; Andrew Ramsay of Dalhousie waited on the Bass with a small, fast boat laden with supplies, packed with reinforcements. Midnight and watchfires burned dim round Dunbar's walls, both navigational aids and a spur for success. Ramsay hoisted anchor and pulled for Agnes. Galleys, Genoese and English, missed him and the solo Scots ship slipped home; his arrival proved decisive.

Captured by pirates!

Later warriors were to hold the Bass but now a king came. James Stewart was too young to rule his own country, too vulnerable to be left alone. Sent to his auld ally, France, James waited on the Bass for a ship. For a month he lived in the castle, enduring the draughts, watching the seals and no doubt dreaming of future glory. Poor young James! When his ferry eventually came it was captured by pirates and the king spent the next fifteen years an English prisoner. He must have had bitter-sweet memories of the snell Forth wind as he lay snug in London Tower.

By the 1670s the fort had cannon ranked behind its curtain wall, cannon on its four towers and a garrison of two dozen. The Bass was an important place, its governor drawing a salary of £1,000, its gannets harvested for food, its mutton exported to England — all in surprising quantity!

But the Bass held more than sheep. Religious wars flared through Scotland as Covenanters strived to establish a Presbyterian Kirk. Hunted and harried, some were hanged, others imprisoned. The Bass was to be a secure jail, home to hardy moor-men and ranting prophet alike. Peden was imprisoned here, and Gibb who led the Bo'ness sweet singers to witness the destruction of Edinburgh for its wickedness, Blackadder and many more. Again psalms rose to rival the gull shriek and pounding sea but Covenanter faith was rewarded with the revolution of 1688. An arrogant James was replaced by a haughty William.

Now it was the Jacobites' turn to be persecuted, but Charles Maitland kept the Stuart flag high above the Bass. A blockade starved him out and the authorities tightened the screw.

A prison for Covenanters then for Jacobites

Where Covenanters had once endured the damp dungeons, now Jacobites jostled in the Bass.

Instead of enduring, the Jacobites rose. June 1691 and the garrison was overpowered, the Rock held again for James. Twenty-one men against a kingdom but France provided a boat and Williamite ships were unsafe in the Forth.

A flotilla was sent in but naval guns proved useless and starvation was tried again. This time the garrison used cunning; spreading all their remaining supplies out, they invited the Commissioner of Estates to dine. Casual mention of surrender resulted in laughter and a request: "What could you possibly offer in return?"

How about a free pardon and passage to France?

"Done!" Easy agreement from starving men. For four years they had held a nation off, now it was time to leave. After the siege the castle was razed and the Bass returned to history's lazy neglect. Now only an unmanned light blinks over waters which once saw bold men.

Dunbar's Black Agnes — and a world prophet

It is unusual to create a harbour by carving through a castle; even more unusual to stand beside that harbour and watch kittiwakes nesting at eye level and within touching distance. But Dunbar is like that. This village thrives on its own originality; there is nowhere quite like it.

Sitting on a curve of coast a few miles south of the Forth, Dunbar has seen kings, queens and a protector, privateers, whalers and fishermen, battles, sieges and smugglers. Just about everything has happened here, from the first battle of the War of Independence to the erection of a Nuclear Power Station.

But amongst the history there has always been nature and Dunbar has combined the two in a fascinating Country Park. It covers 1667 acres stretching west along the coast from Dunbar Castle, and has a variety of birds, plants, cliffs, woodlands and the sea. Always the sea, for the sea has been the lifeblood of Dunbar for centuries. Of course, this is no ordinary park, not in Dunbar. This is the John Muir Country Park and that should be something special.

For years John Muir has been unknown in Scotland, a prophet not without honour save in his own country, for he has certainly been honoured abroad. Dunbar born, Muir was taken to the United States at the age of eleven and only once returned to his birthplace. In between he was busy walking, working, writing. John Muir has been termed the Father of Conservation and thanks to his work the idea of National Parks has spread around the world.

An inveterate wanderer, Muir was intoxicated by the concept of unchallenged wilderness and he spent much of his time in places such as the Yosemite Valley and the Sierra Nevada. By the late 1880s he recognised the irretrievable harm man was doing by exploiting nature and he began to campaign to conserve. His ideas took root and in 1890 the United States gained the first of her National Parks. Muir's concern had helped keep a little of the Earth free from man's destructive encroachment.

In Scotland, John Muir was little thought of; it was not until 1976, 62 years after his death, that the John Muir Country Park was established. A few years later Muir's house at 126/128 High Street was opened as a museum and tribute. Dunbar had fittingly recognised one of her famous sons.

To counterbalance the gentle Muir, Dunbar can boast a warrior female. Black Agnes, the sombre complexioned daughter of Randolph, Earl of Moray, was married to the Earl of March. Left in command of Dunbar Castle, Agnes was confronted by the latest English invading force, led by the Earl of Salisbury. With the blood of her father fierce in her, Agnes slammed shut the gate, manned the parapets and held the red walls of the castle against Salisbury's might.

Six weeks of siege, with mailed men-at-arms clattering through green Lothian, archers exchanging fire and the blue hazed smoke of burning homes a backdrop to disease and valour. And always there was Agnes. "Come they early, come they late, they found Black Agnes at the gate." Agnes on the battlements, dusting the stones to show her contempt for English artillery. Agnes watching as a Scots arrow felled a knight standing beside Salisbury. "Agnes love-shafts go straight to the heart." Agnes causing a great stone to smash an English war engine and sending the men sheltering beneath scurrying for safety. Agnes, always Agnes, and when a ship from the Bass Rock brought provisions and men, Salisbury despaired and withdrew.

It is easy to imagine Agnes, arms akimbo on the castle wall, mocking the English retreat. The east coast wind would flick hair across her face, flutter her long gown, caress the dark complexion with its taunting eyes. She could be there still, a spectre watching over the harbour, the countryside which saw two battles, the sea with its convoys from the Second World War and the Heinkels shot down by the RAF.

Even in its shattered state, the castle provides Dunbar's buckle. Sea and land meet under the fragmented walls, countryside and town merge easily beside the corrugated sandstone. There is still a handful of fishing boats in the harbour but more than a century ago there were hundreds. Up to three hundred in 1819 when the fish were plentiful. Dunbar must have been a lively place when the fleet was in, with the vennels and closes crammed with fisherfolk, boisterous with their salt-tongued voices. As the years slid past Dunbar retained her prosperity, a new harbour being added to accommodate the boats and the castle suffering accordingly. New buildings enhanced the High Street, new hopes for the people. But kismet changed and the fleet dwindled as the century turned and advanced.

Perhaps the old ways were right, certainly the God-fearing blamed the advent of Sunday fishing for the town's decline. Or maybe there were just too many fishing craft off the east coast and the larger boats of other ports took control. Yet there is still fishing from Dunbar, the sea is as important — nearly — as ever and the tang of salt water permeates this bright sandstone town.

Agnes and John Muir would approve; thankfully.

North Berwick, Auld Hornie and a spooky castle tale

From all East Lothian they gathered at the Kirk. Scores of them; some on horseback, some on foot, some who'd crossed the sea on crazy sieves. Ordered by their Maister they came willingly; devilishly keen to obey.

To the thrum of a Jew's harp they danced a wild reel, tossed back the red wine and waited for the ceremony to begin. Inside the Kirk the roll was called by the Maister, the horned and hideous King of Hades, Auld Hornie himself.

It was 1591 and Scotland, as usual, was in turmoil. King James VI was in Denmark courting Anne, his bride, and the Earl of Bothwell saw this as a chance to grab power for himself.

Bothwell was a wicked man with a strong interest in witchcraft and he was probably — but not definitely — the man who ordered all the East Lothian witches to gather at North Berwick that ghastly night.

There was a surprising mixture, from young girls to farmhands to the Prestonpans schoolmaster — although the bairns from his classes might not have been surprised! Each witch was asked how they had tried to bring down the king, and when one man, still red with new-ploughed earth, replied "…. there is naething ails the king yet, God be thankit", the devil forgot himself so much as to strike him a very sublunary blow.

Notwithstanding that not all his congregation were of one mind, Auld Nick hoped to use their collective powers to whistle up a storm which would swamp the king's returning ship. Four graves were desecrated, finger, toe and knee joints being removed to be pulverised for the spell, and the witches kissed the devil's doup in loving farewell.

Like most of Bothwell's plots, the spell failed. Jamie survived the sea passage and lived to be king of both Scotland and England; he took his revenge on the Lothian witches, but Bothwell was not caught. He died years later, a professional conjuror in Europe.

That episode resounded throughout Scotland and perhaps echoes reached William Shakespeare deep in England, but it was the only time North Berwick itself came into national importance. It is a quiet, happy place and probably always was, being off the beaten invasion routes and not strategically important. Perhaps it was for this peaceful atmosphere that St Baldred came in the early 8th century. He might have been a Northumbrian holy man, and as well as living part-time on the Bass, he left his name indelibly on the East Lothian coast.

At that time there was a rock firmly in the centre of the main coastal shipping lane and scores of boats had smacked into it, losing their crews to the waves.

St Baldred was unhappy about this, perhaps thinking that each boatload drowned decreased his flock, and he decided to do something about it. Approaching the rock, he folded his long robes, sat on it and sailed to the shore. Unbelievable? St Baldred's Boat, as the rock became known, can still be seen not far east of Tantallon Castle.

Now, mention of Tantallon could bring in a dozen tales of siege and warfare, of the Douglases and Cromwell, of the old rhyme: 'Din doon Tantallon, mak a brig tae the Bass'. Each statement of which was reckoned impossible. But these stories are all well known. Less celebrated is the last time Tantallon played her part in the history of East Lothian.

The castle was not so ruinous then, weather and time had left still a vestige of shelter in the upper apartments, and bad communications had left the shoulder of East Lothian a backwater.

Shipwrecked to Tantallon!

The 19th century had barely turned when there was a ship wrecked at Fidra and an old sailorman tossed ashore. Life at sea was obviously too dangerous and the survivor decided it might be easier to live off the land. He made his base in the last surviving upper apartment of Tantallon, gathered a heterogeneous crew and plundered round about.

Descending by rope ladder, the old land pirate raided Seacliff, stole from Scoughall and convoyed food from a vessel snugly moored in North Berwick harbour. A gentleman lost both his spyglass and his clothes, others found their larders bare or sheep missing.

Local fishermen were too superstitious to investigate the lights in the castle; they still refused to put to sea if they saw a pig while on their way to the boat, still shunned talking of hares or salmon while at sea, and if they met the minister before setting out they put their caps back to front to deceive the devil as to their direction. Would Bothwell have been so easily fooled?

As so often in Scotland, it took a woman to break the mystery. A bunch of young lassies were under the castle walls thinning turnips when they noticed someone watching them. Not surprisingly they ran, screeching, and a posse of Lothian lads was raised.

Tantallon was besieged for the last time in its history, the old brigand was captured, banished from the district and peace returned.

Today North Berwick sits beneath the conical Law, one of the friendliest resorts in Scotland. Dignified, carrying memories of St Baldred in its street names, vestiges of old days in its ecclesiastical remains, it is a happy place.

But the town does not idly dream of its past. More visitors play golf than ever danced to Bothwell's tune and far more enjoy the beach than ever marched to the red walls of Tantallon.

Cockenzie — the Scots Klondyke!

Following the coast east from Edinburgh there is a succession of historic little towns, each with an individual character.

First comes Musselburgh with its race course and memories of Pinkie, then Prestonpans with the Preston Grange Beam engine and tales of Prince Charlie's '45 battle, and thirdly is Cockenzie and Port Seton.

It is only a small place, usually hurried through because of its vast power station stabbing two chimneys 500 feet into the sky, but there is more to Cockenzie than meets the eye.

It all began at the Boat Shore, *Cul Coinnich,* the Cove of Kenneth, and the fishing. There were always fish in the Forth and fishermen at Cockenzie, but it was not until the later part of the 16th century that Robert, Lord Seton, built a harbour. King

James VI rewarded him by making Cowkany — as it was spelt — a Burgh of Barony, but the Setons and the village were already interdependent.

The very name Seton comes from the Sea Town, the village by the sea, and the Setons had lived here for centuries, as warriors, royalists, politicians and religious benefactors.

By 1670 there was a harbour at Port Seton, too, coalpits and saltpans and a printing works. The place was thriving, with boats trading to the Low Countries and fishermen hauling in their catch. Cockenzie was a Scottish Klondyke.

And then decline set in, with wars and taxes impoverishing the village and Lord Seton a Jacobite exile. His lands were bought by the York Buildings Company of London, who built the first Scottish railway. This ran from Tranent coalpits to Port Seton harbour, had wooden rails and was pulled by horses.

The York Company also founded a glass works, which failed. A family of Haddington merchants, the Cadells, bought into the area and began a salt trade to the Baltic and the German Hanseatic ports.

The salt smugglers!

Salt was heavily taxed and there was a fair bit of smuggling carried on. One particular Cockenzie pair, David Hastie and Jennie Pow, hid their duty-free salt beneath layers of fish in Jennie's cart. Maybe this ploy was too obvious, for they were frequently discovered and fined, but perhaps the money saved by the times they succeeded made up for it.

There was oyster dredging in the Forth, but not for long, and the fishing diminished at the same time. Poverty waited at the sea-wall of Cockenzie, its many barbed claws eager to sink into the fisherfolk. Hardship did not come alone; cholera hit the town and the release of previously bonded colliers led to a rapid decline in moral standards as the barely-educated miners roamed free.

When times are bad the Scots travel. The Cockenzie folk did not emigrate, instead they took to whaling as naturally as to fishing.

Into the Davis Strait and the cruel Arctic, the Cockenzie men roamed, and one particular ship was in Baffin Bay when the ice gripped her fast.

With temperatures permanently plunged to terrifying lows, the crew suffered that winter, but kept alive by faith and fortitude. Daily prayers and discipline saw them through the terrible Arctic night and when the ice slackened the first rescue ship to find them contained the son of one of the stranded men. Family ties were strong in Cockenzie.

There was at least one other rescue attempt by Cockenzie men, when Franklin was lost searching for the fabled North West Passage. Like the others in that tragic episode, it failed. The mystery of Franklin's end has not been totally solved.

Opium Wars!

But the Cadells were characters too. Francis Cadell, Cockenzie born, was an adventurer. He fought in the Opium Wars, wandered in Peru and found fame in Australia.

In 1853 South Australia was being opened up and the Governor offered £4,000, which was a fortune then, to the first captain to sail from the mouth of the Murray to a town many miles upstream. Cadell took up the challenge, sailing with a crew of Cockenzie men and finding he was in a race with a Captain Randell.

Up the sludge green water they went with the sandy bluffs and mournful eucalyptus, the sparse grassland and maybe an odd kangaroo wondering what all the fuss was about. Cadell won by a few hours and spent more time in Australia, but he left there too for the idyllic islands of the Pacific.

Other Cadells were as colourful, like Colonel Thomas Cadell who won the Victoria Cross at the siege of Delhi in 1857, became Chief Commissioner of the Andaman and Nicobar Islands and ended up Provost of Cockenzie in 1904. Sadly, he was the last Cadell of Cockenzie, and Cockenzie House was leased to another explorer, Sir Everard Thurn.

Sir Everard travelled to South America and in Brazil he found Roraima, the extraordinary upheaved plateau which Conan Doyle immortalised in the '*Lost World*' and which was first climbed only a decade or so ago.

Perhaps there was something lingering in the Cockenzie air which helped, the aura of old-time traders, fishermen and whalers permeating the atmosphere.

Bleak moorland that became Portobello

A wild place, the Figgate Muir, bleak moorland, heather and whins. To the north, the grey Forth batters the beach while wind whips the sand into eye-stinging clouds.

The name is old, a modernisation of a Saxon word for a cow-ditch, totally unrelated to present day Portobello. But there were cattle here once, when the monks from the Abbey of the Holy Rood used the area for pasture.

In the high middle ages the monks were a powerful influence in Scotland, their animals transforming the landscape and turning forestland to grasslands. Perhaps it was the monks' sheep that changed this area from part of the hunting forest of Drumsheugh to a moor.

In 1296 the red flare of war burst over the border as Edward Longshanks led his blood-hungry veterans against the untried Scottish spearmen. There was instant disaster for Scotland at

Dunbar, but with the nobility — Scotland's leaders — in disarray, more natural leaders came through.

One was William Wallace and legend tells of him bringing 200 men to Figgate Muir to join other patriots. The long struggle of resistance against the English had a beginning in Portobello, then. But as well as Wallace, Figgate was visited by Cromwell. That was in 1650, again the year of a famous Scottish defeat, and again it was at Dunbar.

Cromwell's army occupied Scotland and this time there was no Wallace. Resistance was sporadic, mainly in the Highlands, and the Roundhead soldiers grew bored.

There were worse garrisons than Edinburgh; the West Indies, for example, or the Cameron country where Lochiel bit the throat out of one of Cromwell's officers, and at least the beer was cheap, if thick.

Still, amusements were sought. In 1661 the puritan roundheads — the men who made New Year a Scottish holiday instead of the more traditional Christmas — marched to the Figgate Muir and cheered a dozen plump females as they raced for a prize of cheese. Portobello was to see other races, a century later, and they were not so innocent. Not even superficially.

Before them came the name. Amazingly it was another war that brought history to Portobello, but this one was fought over a larger area. In 1739 a Glasgow ship's master named Jenkins returned home with his ear pickled in a jar. The Spanish, he claimed, had cut it off.

Caribbean Porto Bello

This was an excellent excuse for war in the touchy 18th century, and the British promptly sent an expedition to the

Spanish Main. Under Admiral 'Old Grog' Vernon the Royal Navy cruised the Caribbean, falling on the gold town of Puerto Bello on the Isthmus of Darien. The town fell, the seamen made prize money and a few actually managed to keep their share. Well, at least one did, George Hamilton, a saddler by trade and he used his pieces of eight to build a small house in the Figgate Muir. He called the house Portobello and the name stuck.

Hamilton kept to his old trade and drummed up custom by offering a saddle as prize in a horse race. It seemed that the Muir attracted racing as easily as warriors, for Hamilton had other, less savoury sports too. There were the Goose Races, for instance, where a goose was hung upside down from a gibbet with grease smeared on its featherless neck. Horsemen thundered past, grabbing at the goose in an attempt to decapitate it.

Even more loathsome was the cat game, when a cat was crammed into a barrel which was hung from a pole. This time the 'sportsmen' had to dislodge the cat into the crowd where it would be grabbed by the tail and thrown high into the air until it died.

There were other sides to the good old days apart from so-called healthy living.

From highwaymen to pleasure

Highwaymen and footpads hung about the moor, the muggers of the 18th century, and Hamilton's Portobello earned a bad reputation.

Very gradually this changed, but not until well into the next century. By then Walter Scott had trained with the yeomanry on Portobello Sands — incidentally writing the *'Lay of the Last Minstrel'* at the same time — and the Annual Carters plays had ended in drunken riots.

But middle class Victorian respectability eroded the adventure of the one-time muir and fine solid houses, Regency and later, rose along the seafront. Pleasure steamers called at the now long-gone pier, bathers used both the sea and the lamented, departed pool, and Portobello became a pleasant place.

As with most villages Portobello had its day and slid downhill, but this slide has passed its nadir. The beach is clean again and to judge Porty's popularity as a resort it is necessary only to visit on a hot summer Saturday.

And even today there is a beauty in a long June evening with the sun setting red higher up the Forth and the little ripples flowing soft and silver up the sand.

Golf and gunfire on Leith Links

It would be as impossible to leave Leith out of any book on the Forth as it would be to tell all — or even half — of Leith's story. The past of a port as diverse as Leith could fill many books, from its trade to its shipbuilding, its glory of once rivalling Edinburgh as Scotland's capital and the privateers who scoured the oceans. Many ports, however, could boast of some of these; few have an area like Leith Links.

Links, in Scotland, will invariably be connected with golf, and golf by the sea. This is correct of Leith as much as anywhere else. Golf was played at Leith when other, supposedly ancient, courses were only sand and turf wastes beside the sea. But before that, or possibly at the same time, Leith's Links were used for less pleasurable pursuits.

Queen Marie, one time wife of James V, mother of the famous Queen Mary and always an underrated personality who pops up unexpectedly in the remarkable pages of sixteenth century history, had individualistic ideas as to her role. Never content to play a shadow to anyone, Marie used French forces to support her adopted Scotland from the always present English threat.

First the French dismissed an English garrison from Inchkeith, then settled down in fortified Leith. The Scots did not like the English, but they were not too keen on the French either, and Knox's budding Protestants put forward a request for their space rather than their presence. Marie, strong willed and Catholic, rejected this and, reading the situation correctly, shifted her court from Holyrood to Leith before the mob came for her.

Fair enough, thought the Protestants and, gathering an embryo army, threw it at the manned walls of Leith. Up against professionals, the half armed rabble had little chance; the French repulsed them and sallied out so the Scots withdrew at speed back to Edinburgh. Marie enjoyed the spectacle.

A siege proved laughable and the English had to be called in for their expertise. Batteries of siege artillery were dragged north and Leith Links were hacked up for the cannon of Somerset and Pelham. This siege proved bloody but successful, both armies left and Scotland was foreigner-free for a while. Apart from bitterness, one legacy was left; two gun emplacements rose proud in the Links for generations of children to play on. The taller was — and hopefully still is — known as the Giant's Brae. It is good for sledging on in winter!

After this, the Links returned — more or less — to their more natural use as a golf course. More or less because there was always the odd duel, execution, cock-fight or invasion by plague victims, but that was secondary. Golf was the main event.

In the past there had been laws passed by the Scots Estates, forbidding the common folk to play golf and ordering them to practise archery instead, but as time passed the nobility saw the fascination of this frustrating game and took it up themselves. James IV was the first recorded king to play, but he was followed by a host of significant Scotsmen.

In 1627 Montrose, later to lead victorious armies, was paying five shillings for his "goffe balls" at Leith Links, and no doubt losing quite a few. Fighting Covenanters was probably easier than sinking long putts! Only a few years later King Charles, Montrose's boss, was playing on the Links when a courier informed him of the rebellion in Ireland. Apparently Charles lost his head, threw down his clubs — his ball must have been lost in the rough — and galloped to the Privy Council for confirmation.

Both Charles and Montrose were to be executed as a result of that rising.

Claret at the 19th!

Better known is James the Seventh's fondness for the game. When playing two English lords at the Links, James chose one Paterson, a shoemaker, as his partner. Whether this was genuine democracy, an attempt to play with an expert or a fit of gamesmanship to upset the haughty nobles is not known. In the event, Paterson and the king won and the shoemaker used his winnings to buy a house in Edinburgh's High Street. Golfer's Land still stands, a memorial to a royal game.

Other golfers who wasted their time in more trivial pursuits were John Porteous (who had a great reputation as a golfer but failed as commander of the city guard) and Forbes of Culloden: 'Great Forbes, patron of the just', who was known to play golf even in thick snow.

At first there was no clubhouse, but the players retired to a tavern in the Kirkgate where they drank thin claret out of pewter tankards. One of the original nineteenth holes!

Newhaven — first new town in Scotland

When King James the Fourth decided he wanted Scotland to be a major naval power, he was being less ridiculous than some historians like to assume.

Scotland had always been blessed with a population who took naturally to the sea; there had never been a lack of skill or enterprise, only of capital. From the leather curraghs of the Picts to the galley fleets of MacDonald, the kiss of salt water had inflamed generations of Scots, but in the closing decades of the 15th century the East coast seamen thrust their way to prominence.

With fighting mariners like Andrew Wood and the Barton family, Scotland had won renown as a seafaring nation and James considered such men should have a ship worthy of them.

Building massive warships was all the rage in Europe and James cast around for a suitable site; he chose the south shore of the Forth a few miles west of Leith. A village, maybe Scotland's original new town, grew up around the dockyards and storehouses of James' ship. Our Lady's Port of Grace,

James called it; more pragmatic, the locals termed it the new haven.

'Michael', the great ship that James built, had a short, tragic life. Like HMS Hood, she did not live up to expectations, and was sold to France shortly after the blood dried on the reeking grass of Flodden. Only one piece of the great 'Michael' can still be seen in Edinburgh, a solid beam which helps support Gladstone's Land in the Royal Mile.

After James' death no more warships were built at Newhaven, but the village did not lose its connection with the sea.

In the ensuing centuries, Newhaven's fishermen were to create a reputation as a breed quite capable of looking after themselves. As far back as 1573, the 'Society of Free Fishermen of Newhaven' existed to uphold their rights.

Their leader was the Boxmaster who managed the strongbox which contained all the society's documentation, as well as the money. Every year the Boxmaster changed, so no one man could be said to rule the fishermen.

Because of the society, certain waters of the Forth, from the Green Scalp of Inchkeith to the beacon ground off Leith's Black Rocks, were reserved exclusively for Newhaven.

This right was defended vigorously, for as well as herring and oysters the Forth yielded salmon and crabs. The herring were first discovered in 1793, just west of Inchcolm, and for the next 150 years they were the mainstay of the Newhaven fishermen.

Oyster wars!

It was the oyster grounds that caused more trouble. With the arrogance of size, Edinburgh permitted outsiders to dredge for oysters in the Newhaven scalps.

Vicious little skirmishes erupted on the choppy waters, with the indignant Newhaven men chasing off the invaders. When detectives were sent to Newhaven to catch the returning boats, the fishwives, as formidable as their men, womanhandled them with some savagery.

These fishwives had a hard life. Expected to bait fishlines and pull an oar as well as lugging a hundredweight of fish to sell in Edinburgh, they dressed in distinctive stripes and could haggle with the single-minded competence of a financier.

Familiar characters in Edinburgh, the fishwives called out their slogans. "Caller Herrin" for fresh herring, "Caller Ou" for oysters and "Caller Parton" for crabs, and were soon surrounded by eager buyers. Oysters sold by the "Long Hundred" — that is, 120 — but schoolboys bought them at a ha'penny a dozen. If the boy was daring, he could offer a kiss in exchange for a 13th.

From time to time plans were submitted to improve Newhaven's facilities.

Just after the Napoleonic Wars there was an upsurge in shipping using Leith and the engineer John Rennie suggested docks should be built at Newhaven. They were not then, but in the 1870s a new harbour was built and soon payment was demanded from the fishermen. Not surprisingly, they were reluctant to pay and the police were called to enforce the law.

The lawmen attempted to grab a fishing boat and there was a scuffle with police and fishermen splashing noisily into the Forth. In the meantime, the Superintendent of Leith Docks was being quietly beaten up. Happy times at the Port of Grace.

As well as a harbour, Newhaven once owned a chain pier which was built in 1821 for vessels plying between Edinburgh and ports up the Forth. For years this pier brought prosperity to Newhaven; a hotel was needed to cater for the crowds and craft going as far upstream as Stirling stopped here.

Unfortunately, as the century wore on the traffic was diverted to Granton and the pier was utilised only by swimmers. Then, in 1898 came a storm, the pier was swept away and Newhaven was purely a fishing port again.

Nowadays very few fishermen make their living from the Forth. There is a public house at the spot where the chain pier touched the shore and the old village of Newhaven has been restored. There are no more fishwives along Edinburgh's Royal Mile and the oyster beds are long since ruined by pollution.

Caer Avon (Cramond) — fort by the river

Select could be used to describe Cramond, or perhaps exclusive. It is certainly picturesque, a secluded hamlet set beside the mouth of a river, proud of its own beach, its sculled ferry, its shapely island and treacherous causeway. Even if this was all Cramond had, it could relax in satisfaction, for to have retained so much within minutes of hustling Edinburgh is to have achieved something notable. There is nowhere comparable in Scotland.

But there is more to Cramond than surface-deep appearance. The character of the village was forged young, when living men had seen Christ and the stones of Hadrian's Wall were yet unquarried. It was the Romans who recognised the value of this sheltered place, but the Celtic people who named it: *Caer Avon*, the fort by the river. They must have been in awe of the grim, iron men of the 2nd Legion, fearful of the short stabbing swords and convex shields. There would have been galleys here with their oars banked to skiff by the mole, and bare footed seamen from the Tyrrhenian and Adriatic would patter over the foreshore in search of a tavern. The Romans too, would have lived on their nerves, for across the grey Forth was untamed Pictland — and if the turf wall of Antonine was breached! A barbaric eruption of unimaginable horror — the Romans would keep watch on the waters and sharpen their swords regularly.

When the last galley sped away, dimness descended on the

old military station. Minor kingdoms rose and fell, leaving little more than echoes to tell of the centuries of strife which forged the nation state of Scotland.

There is the legend of the eleventh century battle when a Constantine fought a Malcolm for the Scottish throne. The outcome was decided by a typical Forth wind which blasted sand into the faces of Constantine's forces. Perhaps now, perhaps later, the fighting days passed and the Almond flowed sweetly toward the humped island, ungreased with the blood of slaughtered men.

Instead there came titles, boats and industry. Baroness Cramond, wife to an English Chief Justice, provided the title, with her sons and grandsons to maintain the name, but she owned no land in the village and did nothing to help it prosper. Industry introduced the boats; an ironworks brought employ-ment and a handful of sloops rode to anchor where Roman galleys once had bobbed. Arrogant Ironmasters supervised their loading while whaups pecked on the muddy foreshore beneath; a strange site for industry.

Mangled on Cramond Brig!

Upstream is Old Cramond Brig with a story which could be told only of a Scottish king. The monarch was James the Fifth whose reign lacked the glamour of his daughter Mary and the glory of his Flodden-felled father, but which had its own character. This James used his Stewart charm on the not unwilling womanhood of Scotland, adding to the Royal population, but no doubt losing the love of sundry parents!

It could have been in this role, or as his *alter ego* of 'The Gudeman of Ballengeich' that King James appeared on Cramond Brig, unescorted and, apparently, unrecognised. A lone stranger in the early decades of the sixteenth century was anybody's target, and James was soon attacked by a bunch of thugs. No doubt he fought, for his father's blood was strong in him, but he was in danger of being overpowered when a gallant rescuer crunched along the cobbles. Not a white chargered knight, but Jock Howison the miller, armed with a most useful flail.

With the muggers mangled, Jock helped the dazed stranger on his journey — any female companion having doubtless fled — and was rewarded by lands round about. There was a condition of course; any visiting monarch had to be fed and watered. This agreement has been kept by both sides, even if the story might be a little elaborated.

The buttressed bridge is still there, as safe to walk along as it ever was in James' time, but there are no handy millers threshing corn to hail, only traffic from the nearby A90.

Whale blown up on Cramond Island!

Other visitors have added colour to Cramond. One thousand troopers were quartered here during the troubles of the mid seventeenth century, and a whale was blown up on Cramond Island in 1769. Whales are rare in the Forth, although seals and sharks can still be caught off Dunbar, so for a while the fifty foot carcass proved popular. No doubt the smell was little to a populace used to the 'Gardyloo!' of Auld Reekie!

Not only whales have been stranded on the island; people are regularly stuck here. There is a causeway at low tide, with a notice warning of the only times to cross, but people find the island so delightful they tend to linger. The lifeboat provides something like a ferry service in summer, rescuing the unwary. The other ferry is across the Almond; an open boat. The far side of the river is idyllic, a tree lined beach with an eagle carved rock, the phantom hound of Barnbougle and Queensferry as an eventual destination — only the tanker terminal at Hound Point reminds of the realities of life. And even that is fascinating in incomparabe Cramond.

Inchkeith — isle of the living dead!

Easily the most prominent island in the Forth, Inchkeith has a history which stretches into Celtic mysticism. In the Dark Ages, when merging tribesmen were founding their nations and Scotland was the meeting place of religions in elemental opposition, the small islands provided both a refuge and a power point for the warring sides. Inchkeith was no except-ion.

Like all the major Forth islands, Inchkeith had her saint, but before Adamman set his apocryphal foot on the rocky, fertile surface, the island had its own unique spiritualism. Most of the tales have been lost now and even the memory has hazed to near oblivion, but the name *Caer Guidi* — coined by Bede — remains, and a shadowy fragment of the island as a lost Celtic city. An other world perhaps? An Eastern *Tir nan Og?* Not for the Gaelic speaking Dalriads of Argyll, but the Picts of Fife and the Britons of Lothian. A central point between two analgous cultures disrupted by Roman galleys?

There could have been kelpies here, in the days when Fife was densely wooded and the Forth a frontier between Roman and freedom, or perhaps they were only seals, like the ubiquitous mermaids of Scottish waters.

Enigmatic, Inchkeith remained. At the beginning of the eleventh century the Vikings were the enemy and in a battle fought in Angus a warrior named Robert distinguished himself.

Malcolm the Second rewarded him with the lands of Keith —
and the island in the Forth, now and forever Inchkeith. With its
strategic position midway between Fife and Lothian, Inchkeith
should have been a significant prize in the early English wars,
but perhaps English naval power was too predominant for this
scrap to matter;   later this island would see its share of
bloodshed and powdersmoke.

In the meantime Kings and Councillors created other uses
for Inchkeith. Mediaeval Scotland, in common with the rest of
Europe, periodically endured the plague. Virtually incurable, it
led to a disgusting death and spread swiftly. The only treatment
was isolation, normally on the Burgh Muir outside Edinburgh
but occasionally the Forth islands were used.   During the
outbreak of 1497 the Privy Council ordered the plague stricken
to assemble on Leith Sands, from where they would be rowed
to Inchkeith.

On a raw winter day with the wind howling from the east and
sleet jammering from the rocks, the poor victims must have
yearned for death. Inchkeith would have been a desperate
place then.

Just as desperate, if the story can be believed, was the dumb
nurse James the Fourth marooned on the island. A man of
infinite interests, James wanted to experiment with language
and, unlike most he had the power to pursue his preoccup-
ations. Picking up a pair of orphans, the king had them sent to
Inchkeith in the care of the dumb nurse. His object was to hear
which language the children eventually spoke;   rumour
claimed they spoke Hebrew. Rumour was probably wrong.

When the sixteenth century growled to its bitter middle
decades, warfare returned to the Forth.   No longer purely
political, wars revolved round religion and former foes found
themselves friends, auld allies adversaries. This series of wars
started in the usual way, with an English army ravaging on land,
English ships plundering the Forth and Scots forces resorting
to guerrilla warfare. With a fleet of twenty five ships, the English

navy failed to land at St Monace but garrisoned Inchkeith instead. It must have been a popular posting — a tiny islet separated from hostile shores by only a couple of miles of water! Even so, the Scots needed help to retake it. At this stage of the fighting, the French were still friendly, and it was an Italian/French/Scottish force which landed to expel the English. There was severe fighting, with one of the famous Strozzis falling and the English withdrawing very gradually to the higher northern end of the island. It is easy to imagine the hoarse yells, roar of arquebuses and clatter of swords as the allies pressed their way to gradual victory.

Surrender!

Not so long after, the confused Scots wondered what it was all about. Now the French refused to leave the island and Elizabeth's help had to be sought — religious wars seemed to be like that! Sixteen English ships tossed on the steep Forth waves until the French surrendered, but by now the Scots had seen enough of fortified islands and destroyed the defences.

There were no more battles on Inchkeith and the island suffered between alternate periods of fortification and desolation, with an occasional visit by plague victims. No Scottish government seemed to use the island and it was not until the late nineteenth century that an apprehensive Westminster turned the place into a miniature Maginot Line. By that time, of course, the Royal Navy was the most powerful in the world and there was slender prospect of any enemy fleet penetrating the Forth — but Governments never seem to be practical.

After a period of defensive readiness against the Germans the island again sits astride the seaways, visited by few and home to none. Inchkeith waits for another use.

Forth Rail Bridge.

The Forth Bridges from Fife.

Sunset over the Forth Road Bridge.

The Forth Bridges from the air.   (Photo by The Daily Mail).

North Berwick from The Whale's Jaw.

Bass Rock.

Aberdour, the railway station.

The Old Pier, Aberdour.

North Berwick, the beach and Berwick Law.

The beach and harbour, Kinghorn.

Cellardyke Harbour.

The "Robinson Crusoe" statue, Largo, Fife.

Crail, the Tolbooth.

North Berwick, the golf course and Bass Rock.

The harbour, Leith.

Inchcolm Island from the golf course, Aberdour.

Five thousand men to build the Forth Rail Bridge!

The year was 1890 and the spectators held their breath. Beneath them the grey Forth was feathered by a breeze, beside them throbbed the latent power of a laden locomotive. One or two shivered, a few gnawed nervous lips, some sipped whisky from silver flasks. In front of them was a sonnet in steel, a structure so revolutionary that it was unimaginable — but it was there, joining the south shore of the Forth to Fife. A bridge across the Forth where a ferry had operated for centuries, and the Prince of Wales here to open it.

But — and here was the rub — there was doubt about safety. Only eleven years before there had been celebrations about another engineering triumph, but the mighty Tay Bridge had collapsed in a storm, killing scores. This time there would be no chances taken; the Forth Bridge would be proven safe before the first passenger touched it with a tentative foot.

At a given signal the locomotive began to move, two engines pulling heavy carriages, a third engine pushing at the rear. A mile and a half to the north a similar train was also moving, steam clouding onto the new painted steel. As the engines rolled onto the bridge there was a shudder from the crowd, not the structure, and an apprehensive gasp. This was the moment of truth, the time they had dreaded and worked for. Disaster or triumph as eighteen hundred tons of machinery rumbled above the Forth.

For hundreds of years the southern and northern shores of the Forth had been connected by ferries. Queensferry had been a geographical must as a crossing point, a spot where both coasts came close; above here was the Firth of Forth, beneath was the Scottish Sea or Scotswater. The Romans, of course, had recognised the strategic value but it was not until a Saxon refugee became a Scottish queen that recorded history began. Margaret it was who fled from the wrath of the Normans and landed stormbound in free Scotland. She met and married Malcolm, King of Scots, who let her feminine hands alter the Celtic character of his nation with subtle arrogance. The Culdee church was diminished and Papal Rome took its place; feudalism was encouraged and the very Gaelic language began its long recession. She was to be known as Saint Margaret, yet she introduced an alien system that bred bloodshed; she also altered the communications map.

Queensferry and the pilgrims

In Dunfermline lay the Black Rood, rumoured to be a fragment of the True Cross, and Margaret, perhaps in an attempt to soften the savagery of her adopted country, perhaps to make it more acceptable to the rest of Europe, introduced pilgrimages to the shrine. Hospices — mediaeval hotels — were built on either shore of the Forth and between them a free ferry plied for the pilgrims. The Queensferry was born and named with all the veiled politics of royal patronage.

From rowing boat to sailing craft the centuries were marked by the continual passage of people. The men of North Queensferry gained sole rights as ferrymen, an early example of a closed shop. No man born beyond Ferryhills could row on the passage but perhaps that was a double edged sword.

David the First put the ferry on a regular basis under the Abbot of Dunfermline and prices fluctuated so much that a fee had to be agreed; so much for free passage! In 1474 passengers had to pay one Scots penny — and twopence for their horse. They also had to endure the rough tongue of the ferrymen; in centuries of progress that was something which did not change.

Boarding the boat was often by means of a long slippery plank, and the passage time depended on the weather. It would be no joke to be stuck in mid-Forth in an open boat with a raw wind biting through thin clothes and the waves breaking rough all around. Of course, there was no real alternative.

On the other shore, South Queensferry prospered. Between the water and the hills, the main street had to be long and narrow, with high buildings and a sense of isolation. The Dunfermline monks had land there, and there was a fourteenth century Carmelite chapel, but an attempt by a group of Lombards to found a trading post was quelled. Too much competition, claimed the Edinburgh merchants, and nullified the venture.

With people passing through, there had to be an Inn, natural successor to the decaying hospice. South Queensferry had, among others, the Hawes Inn, immortalied by both Scott and Stevenson and still standing proud. By 1800 North Queensferry had a lucky thirteen and within a decade there were substantial piers in both villages. Already, though, there were ominous mutterings about a bridge across the Forth. Thomas Telford, the greatest civil engineer of his day, had prepared plans nearly half a century before and with no current war to drain the nation's finances a bridge was possible.

With the pen of Walter Scott awakening the world to the potential of Scotland, eyes and tourists were turning north; influential travellers demanded more than an open boat. The ferrymen obliged. Steam powered craft churned their paddles on the Forth as different companies competed for custom. A bridge over the Forth? Impossible! And the ferrymen continued their old habits. Sometimes it was not a pleasant experience to sail the Forth; if a man let his dog run free he was likely to be asked, "Hey; do you belong to that dug?" Politely of course.

Inevitably, progress came. As Railway Barons made huge profits — and spectacular losses — the double steel lines streaked north. They halted at Granton, resumed at Burntisland and in between was the world's first rail ferry. It was not enough; there had to be a bridge.

Code of the 'Briggers'

For seven years workmen laboured above the Forth. Sir John Fowler and Sir Benjamin Drake took the credit, but the real builders were the 5000 strong army of 'Briggers'.

They were hard men from every quarter of Britain, drinking men who commuted to work from Edinburgh, Dunfermline and Inverkeithing and who lived in specially built houses in Queensferry itself. Like the Navigators of earlier years, their onset would be feared by many but welcomed by publicans and shopkeepers. Briggers had their own uniform, trousers as bell-bottomed as a seaman's and a broad ring of Forth Bridge steel on their finger. In case of arrest, all contributed to a fund which would pay court fines — Briggers insurance policy — but they worked hard and with skill.

Although Drake and Fowler's design was a cantilever bridge based on a Far Eastern principle, the Briggers had to contend with all the local problems. Not once did they fail, although working hundreds of feet above the water. Conquering the Forth took its toll; fifty Briggers died, ten times that number were injured.

The statistics are formidable; two main spans of over 1700 feet, an overall length of over a mile and a half, a height of 361 feet. When, on that day in 1890, the two trains passed each other and growled on, the Briggers must have thought it worth while. Mingled with the pride, however, would have been a tinge of sadness, and of doubt. Where would the next job come from?

As soon as the Forth Bridge opened, the races began. With the time sliced on the East Coast main line, trains thundered to beat each other's records. It was like the Clyde ferries but with the bonus of a three million pound bridge as a stage. Victorians loved competition; they thrived on it.

So had the ferry operators, but now there were few left. The survivors touted for new business and soon found it in the ever increasing road traffic. Again it was boom time for the ferries and the decree was for larger and faster vessels. Even then there were long queues at the terminals, delays in journeys north and south, detours to Stirling for the lowest bridging point on the Forth.

Bridge was Nazi target!

Public demand led to a public meeting presided over by J Inglis Kerr, Scotland's pioneer of road transport. A Road Bridge was now a must — and one was duly opened. At Kincardine, farther up the Forth. Plans continued, however, until Hitler's war disrupted the flow and Nazi warplanes raided the Forth. The Bridge was Goering's target and the scene of a vicious little battle; it had already seen the Royal Navy's might in World War One as Rosyth developed to meet the North Sea threat. Hurricanes and Heinkels snarling over the Forth and the Navy perfecting its skills beneath the steel spans of the briggers' creation.

With the end of war, arguments began again over a road bridge. A mere ten years later the Ministry of Transport decided that either a bridge or a tunnel should be begun before the end of the decade, and three years later the first pile was driven.

Seven years and twenty million pounds later the bridge was completed, a slenderly elegant suspension bridge which complements its neighbour's chunkiness. The official opening was on September 4, 1964. There can be few sights in the world to match the two Forth Bridges, few journeys as thrilling as a trip over either.

Yet the work still continues. Some 7000 gallons of paint are used to protect the mighty Rail Bridge, and every three years the work begins again. The Road Bridge has to be resurfaced for

the continual river of traffic and in high winds its swing is
commented on. To many, these bridges rival Edinburgh Castle
in symbolising Scotland, and perhaps Saint Margaret would be
proud to look down and see her chosen route so honoured.

Secrets of the wee islands

A seascape without islands is a joyless thing for, like
mountains, islands attract and hold the imagination. Anything
can happen on an island, they are miniature kingdoms where a
man — or a woman — can live in peace with himself and
creation. Robinson Crusoe — whose original came from the
Forth — could be called the father of our modern desire for
island life, but the tales go far beyond that. Brendan the Gaelic
traveller was an inveterate island hopper, but he was only
following an old Celtic custom; half the islands of Britain can
boast a Celtic saint or a ruined chapel! And even before that,
the Odyssey concerns a myriad islands and as many
adventures.

> In the Forth there are ten islands:
> 'Inchgarvie, Mickery, Colm, Inchkeith,
> Cramond, Fidra, Lamb, Craigleith;
> Then round the Bass to the Isle of May
> and past the Carr to St Andrew's Bay.'

Some of these are large enough to yield a long history, others
little more than weed covered rocks. Most lie alone today, a few
are still actively used. The main islands have been dealt with
elsewhere; this section is about the smaller islands, starting
with Craigleith.

Just offshore from North Berwick, Craigleith is about twenty
acres of barrenness with a forbidding, if low, cliff all around.

Unusually for a Forth island, Craigleith does not seem to have any recorded history; it is just there, waiting to be used. Only the seabirds live here, although it would make a good viewpoint for the Forth.

Lamb is just next door, an equally bleak neighbour. Farther to the west, and much more interesting, is Fidra. For years owned by the Northern Lighthouse Board, this fifteen acres islet now belongs to the RSPB — and the birds the society protects. There are hundreds of these, including breeding pairs of eider ducks and nesting seabirds. Fidra would be worth a visit for the birds alone, but it also has a history.

A Celtic chapel was set up on this island, and there was a ferry here from the Abbey of Eldbottle — which seems to have been caught in the wastage of time! The chapel itself was Romanised by William the Lion in 1165, granted to Dryburgh Abbey and used for pilgrimages. And why not? An excellent place to travel to, then and now.

More interesting perhaps is the notion that Robert Louis Stevenson is said to have been inspired by Fidra to write Treasure Island, but that is said about at least two other islands in Scotland. However, Stevenson did stay for a while in North Berwick and the Admiral Benbow could be an Inn from that town.

Farther up yet and north of Cramond is Inchmickery. Save for being a hazard for shipping, this island has a history little more barren than its own grazing. A low island, it has a mysterious monolith on a southern ledge. Who raised the fourteen foot high stone here, and why? Is it Pictish or older? Was this island sacred even before Inchcolm? An intriguing island, Inchmickery, and the scene of rivalry in the nineteenth century. Fishermen from Cockenzie battled with boats from Newhaven to secure the rich oyster beds around the island. Honours were probably about even, but pollution and over dredging — by neither village — spoiled the ground eventually.

Last of the islands is Inchgarvie. This once proud place has the privilege of supporting a column of the Forth Bridge, some might say a sad fate for an island which once held a king's garrison.

That was during the troubled times when Cromwell's war spilled north of the Cheviots and philabeg-clad Highlanders faced the dour Covenanters through powder smoke. A company of musketeers held Inchgarvie for Charles, but General Lambert forced them out in the name of strait-laced parliament.

There had been another garrison, when the French held Inchgarvie soon after Flodden, and the island had also been a state prison and a sanctuary for plague victims. Today it is hardly seen and virtually ignored — but probably plays a more important part than any other Forth island; imagine the Firth without the bridge?

Mass slaughter at Inverkeithing

"**S**ir Hector Roy, the Stout Maclean,
Fought, one to ten, but all in vain,
His broad claymore unsheathing;
Himself lay dead 'mid heaps of slain
For Charles at Inverkeithing."

"Another for Hector!" and the tartan clad youth fell, broadsword clattering onto blood-smeared grass. There had been eight of them, eight bold Macleans of the same family, and all had died before the numberless swords of Cromwell's Ironsides. A section of the Scottish army, they had marched to defend their King, the Scone-crowned Charles, and had met the larger Parliamentary force on the shores of the Firth of Forth.

The slaughter had been immense as the Macleans were

separated from the bulk of the Royalist army, outnumbered and systematically cut down. Sir Hector of Duart was their chief, the father of their clan, and they died to grant him life. One after another, a father and seven sons, they yelled 'Another for Hector' as they fell. Eventually Sir Hector was killed, but the legend of his clansmen's loyalty at the battle of Inverkeithing lives on.

A millennium and a half before the Macleans found their fame, another warrior arrived at Inverkeithing. This was Agricola, on his march north to subdue the Caledonians, forerunners of the Picts. For ten years the Romans camped at the mouth of the Keithing burn, as their legions defeated Calgacus at Mons Graupius, but the attempted conquest of the wild hill lands failed. Inverkeithing would be very much a frontier garrison, with untamed tribes on all sides and soldiers' stories of the fighting circulating rapidly. Peshawar during Victoria's reign, or Dodge City, probably had similar tales and similar people.

Yet a third fighting man was involved in this burgh when William the Lion granted Inverkeithing its charter. That was in 1165, and the town began to grow. Like most Fife coastal towns, Inverkeithing depended on the sea for its prosperity and fame. One of her most renowned sons was an Admiral, but not of Scotland, nor indeed Britain.

Samuel Greig was born in Inverkeithing High Street in 1735 and soon proved that he had the Scottish disease of itchy feet. Following so many Scots, Greig moved east, ending up in Russia. His nautical skill caught the Czar's fancy and Samuel Greig began his ascent.

Founder and Supreme Admiral of the Imperial Russian Navy (although John Paul Jones is a rival for the first claim!), Greig is nearly forgotten in his own country. He is in good company; Scotland has also forgotten Forth born Cochrane who founded the navy of Chile, and Sinclair of Roslin who might have reached the New World a century before Columbus. Like them,

Greig was no paper Admiral; his Scots officered fleet sailed from its Baltic base to the Levant to take on — and defeat — the Turks.

Murder most foul

Not far from Inverkeithing is Donibristle, home to one of the best known lines of Scots dramatic verse, but few could explain anything about the events which gave rise to it. The Bonnie Earl of Moray has a place in folk lore for being murdered, but it was no casual killing.

The year was 1592 and young Moray was rumoured to be very friendly with the queen; he was also son-in-law of the late Regent and had crossed the Gordon Earl of Huntly.

Three excellent reasons to have the man arrested — and who better as lawman than Huntly himself? According to the ballad, Huntly was forbiddden to kill the young Earl: according to history he did so gleefully in one of the most publicised of all Scotland's many noble murders.

Knowing Moray was at Donibristle, Huntly set off to hunt him down. Giving his destination as the horse racing at Leith, Huntly crossed the Forth at Queensferry and promptly put a guard on the boat. He could not be followed, nor could his prey escape that way. With forty men at his heels, Huntly galloped to Donibristle but found the gates well locked.

Burning down houses was nothing to a sixteenth century earl and soon Donibristle was ablaze. Sheriff Dunbar of Moray, left as a decoy, was butchered, and the Earl of Moray slid out a side door and ran to the shore. On a dark February night the Earl had a chance to hide, but a string on his hood was smouldering and the Gordons followed the light. There was a hacking, slashing attack, with Huntly reserving the final stab for himself, but Moray died game. His last comment was sardonic. "You hae spoilt a better face than yer ain", he Is reported as saying, putting a brave light on a sordid story. And Huntly? King James was so displeased with his earl that he threw him into Edinburgh Castle for an entire week.

"Half ower, half ower to Aberdour"

Part of the golden fringe of Fife's beggar's mantle, Aberdour sits at the head of one bay and overlooks another.

It is a neat, friendly village with the settled aura of maturity and solid houses which could be owned by retired Admirals.

The sea dominates here, but the fertile Fife farmland is never far away; the two complement each other. Forth breezes are more refreshing than cold as they whisper through the trees and lift spindrift from the tops of chopped waves.

Possibly the chief glory of Aberdour itself is Silver Sands Bay, a pleasing stretch of beach which is extremely popular when the Scottish sun struggles through, shouldering aside the often looming cloud. It is sheltered here, with the Point of Hawkcraig to the west and Ross Point to the east, while out to sea there is the prospect of the Common Rocks, Inchkeith and the fascinating Inchcolm.

Thousands of people have enjoyed the Silver Sands, but only one has been recorded in verse. Patrick Spens was here when he was ordered to Norway to bring home a princess for the King of Scots — then residing in Dunfermline, a few miles inland. But Sir Patrick returned in the jaws of a storm and was drowned.

> *"Half ower, half ower to Aberdour,*
> *'tis fifty fathoms deep.*
> *And there lies gude Sir Patrick Spens*
> *Wi' the Scots lords at his feet."*

He was not the only mariner to suffer from the fury of the east coast waters, for others were to find the Forth itself more than they could handle.

The sands were also a resting place for pilgrims journeying to the Abbey of St Colm, and Inchcolm and Aberdour are inextricably linked. Inchcolm has been a holy place at least since the days when a Culdee hermit set himself up as a missionary here. Colm, of course, is Callum, the given name of Saint Columba, and it was in his name that the Dalriadic missionaries arrived.

Legends abound, like the story of the Vikings, defeated in battle, paying to have their dead buried on this island, close to heaven.

Or the time King Alexander the First was caught in a Forth squall and sheltered in the curving bay here — not realising he was so close to the island. In gratitude for his deliverance, and for the hospitality shown to him by the Culdee, Alexander founded an Augustinian Abbey. Unfortunately this foundation did not help the Celtic church but drove a small but significant nail into its half-formed coffin.

Double cross at Mortimer's Deep

But the legend best remembered tells of the knight, Sir Alan de Mortimer, who granted St Colm's Abbey the western half of all his lands, provided he could be buried on Inchcolm. The monks agreed, took their new land and waited. When Sir Alan at last died, his body was placed in a lead coffin which in turn was loaded on board a barge.

The barge set off, probably from Aberdour's Silver Sands, but half way across, the crew of 'wicked monks' slid the coffin into the sea. Today the strait between Braefoot Bay and Inchcolm is still known as Mortimer's Deep.

Other items have descended to help litter the bed of the Forth: there was the English pirate, for instance, who pillaged Inchcolm of its treasure. There are those, remembering the story of Mortimer, who would say that the monks deserved to be pirated, but Saint Columba was not one of them.

He watched from above, whistled up a gale and sank the Englishman's ship. That treasure joined Sir Alan on the Forth bed.

But the English returned. During the fourteenth and fifteenth centuries their ships were constantly looting Inchcolm. They came in 1335 and 1336, again in 1384 when they tried a diversion at Queensferry but were driven off. Again in 1421, when the canons had to flee the island for their lives. Perhaps the monks did not flee for long, for that same year brings the tale of the supply ship which was crewed by oarsmen who liked their tipple. When the boat capsized, only Saint Columba could save them, and of course he did!   The food was lost though.

Redbeard's hidden castle treasure

As well as Inchcolm's treasure there is one in Aberdour Castle — once owned by Mortimer. This one was collected by James Douglas, 4th Earl of Morton and Regent of Scotland in the troubled times between the exit of Mary and the entrance of the sixth King James.

A redbearded, pouch-eyed monster, Morton gripped Scotland in a stranglehold and used his clansmen to tighten the noose. He owned Aberdour Castle and must have sat on the chilled ramparts, glaring over the Forth towards Edinburgh and beyond, or at the not-now sacred Abbey of St Colm. By 1578 the Abbey had expired with the onslaught of the Reformation and all the island was good for was as a refuge for plague-stricken ships.

Morton was a leader of the Reformation, a man in the mould of Knox. He may have hidden his wealth somewhere beneath the draughty walls of Aberdour Castle, and what more romantic place could there be? Tales of pirate gold in the West Indies pale when confronted by this phantom-haunted castle opposite the eastern rival to Iona!

A castle and an abbey, two of Scotland's more interesting ruins, but there is one notable building which has been well restored.

St Fillan's church — Fillan being another in the catalogue of Gaelic saints — is as old as the abbey and was worshipped in continuously for nearly seven centuries. In 1796 it was abandoned and the weather worked its way into the stones, tearing, wearing down, until 1926 when the minister, Rev Doctor Robert Johnstone, started to restore it. Now the church stands secure, an entrancingly celestial building and a treasure as significant as any in Aberdour's past.

In common with other Forth islands, Inchcolm suffered a garrison during the war years. There was a battery here during the Kaiser's War, guns trained ready to repel the Imperial German Navy should they dare to try conclusions with the fleet in Rosyth. Fortunately, they never did — Heligoland Bight and Jutland saw to that. It seems a pity to sully the sanctified island with warlike material, but better that than to have German shells whistling down — perhaps Saint Columba could have been asked for a gale.

Inchcolm can still be visited, and there is a custodian on the island to keep the abbey tidy. It is not just a museum, however, for couples can still sail here to be wed, under the watchful eyes of the saints, and the jealous glint of Mortimer who never made it.

Death at Kinghorn sparks 100 year war

It was a howling night in March, waves smashing against the harsh rocks of the coast of Fife.

The lone horseman plodded along the cliff-top, his richly embroidered cloak tugged by the wind. His last host, the master of Inverkeithing Salt Works, had advised him not to continue, but the horseman had laughed and ridden on.

He was journeying to the royal castle at Kinghorn where his wife, the Queen, was waiting for him, but husband and wife were destined never to reunite. A blast of wind, more ferocious than any previous, caught the king as he reached the top of the cliff; his horse reared, the king slipped, crashed over the cliffs and died.

The year was 1286 and the king was Alexander the Third. Some said he deserved to die for feasting in Lent, others mourned, a few remembered the prophecy of Thomas the Rhymer: 'Alas for tomorrow, a day of calamity and misery. Before the 12th hour shall be the sorest wind and tempest that ever was heard of in Scotland.'

To call the aftermath of Alexander's death a tempest was an understatement, for waiting beyond the Tweed were the powerful English, always ready to exploit a weakness — and a mediaeval state without a king was very vulnerable.

The war which followed the king's death at Kinghorn lasted, with breaks, for a century; for some people it has never satisfactorily finished .... there are still Englishmen who are deluded into thinking of Scotland as merely an English province, and there are many Scots who would delight in nullifying the Treaty of Union, thinking it an act of treason. However, among all the horrendous devastation of war, legends tell of at least one family who benefited by Alexander's demise.

Outlawed and destitute, Murdoch Shanks was the Kinghorn man who found the king's body lying behind a 'black stane'. He was rewarded with lands inside the village, and his descendants lived there for centuries. Perhaps there are still Shanks in Kinghorn who can trace their ancestry back.

Interestingly, the name Kinghorn owes nothing to Alexander, or to any other king. It is an Anglified corruption of the Gaelic term for either the Blue Head or the Head of the Corner; yet royalty did stay here.

This was a hunting area for the Scots kings and their castle, convenient for the palace at Dunfermline, was built on a height later to be known as Crying Hill.

Again the meaning is unclear. It is unlikely that a man stood here to watch for fish shoals and the turning tide before crying down to the town below; yet could it be true that this is where travellers hailed the ferry? For Kinghorn was the Fife port for the Broad Ferry for Leith and Newhaven.

Ferries across the Forth

At one time there were three ferries across the Forth; North Berwick to Crail (for St Andrews), Leith to Kinghorn and the Queensferry. By the early 19th century the North Berwick ferry had disappeared and the Queensferry was only challenged by the 'Kinghorn Boat', a sloop manned by four sardonic mariners.

It could not have been a popular passage, starting with a wait of anything up to three days at the Inn, then a hazardous balancing act along a narrow gangplank from shore to boat (walking the plank, in local parlance!) and finally the crossing itself. This could take between one and six hours, depending on the weather — nearly twice the time the MacBrayne ferry takes between Ullapool and Stornoway!

Within a few years a coach was rattling to Kinghorn and the ferry became known as the 'Coach Boat'. It was still open, still with the taciturn, derisive crewmen, but larger, so at low tide it could only be reached by a skiff. The gangplank would not be missed.

There is an element of the Scottish genius for self-destruction in Kinghorn being where the first screw ferry for the Queensferry was built. Launched in the mid-1870s, 'John Beaumont' continued the suicidal streak by sinking in December, 1878, when her master smacked her against the pier at North Queensferry.

Disappointed but not defeated, 'John Beaumont' 's owners salvaged her and she was soon churning the Forth again, but with paddles instead of screws.

Now no ferries cross the Forth and all traffic thunders over the two bridges high above the Queensferry. Where Alexander's body was found now rears a Celtic cross, ignored by most of the vehicles which whizz past.

The castle where the king's wife waited has gone; not a vestige remains, but Kinghorn still clusters at the curve of the coast, unconcerned at the lack of a king.

Alexander of Largo — the real Crusoe

There is a man, standing, dressed in goatskins and peering wistfully out to sea. He is a tall man, bearded and forlorn. For the last hundred years he has stood there, frozen in time while cold winter blasts hurl salt air at him. That would not concern this man, his statue or his person, for the effigy is of Alexander Selkirk, who lived and died a seaman.

Immortalised as Robinson Crusoe, Selkirk's life was as fascinating as the pseudonym Defoe created, if not quite the figure of moral rectitude. He was a Largo man, born in the house behind the statue, and, like a lot of Fifers, exchanged a home life for the sea at an age his mother would consider too young. In view of events, she was right; it was the back end of the seventeenth century and buccaneers brawled over the oceans. Selkirk joined them and cruised to the South Seas. Here he disagreed with the ship's master over the safety of their vessel. The master denied the vessel was unsafe and marooned the mariner on a lonely island.

As his ship hoisted anchor and left, Selkirk roared to be forgiven and let back on board — he was better on Juan Fernandez. The ship sank.

Years later, a tiny squadron crept onto Selkirk's island, loosed anhcor and sent a boat ashore. That boat, and the next, did not return and fearing a Spanish ambush an armed expedition assaulted the island. They returned with Alexander Selkirk and his story; for four years he had lived alone with the goats and his Bible, he had nearly forgotten how to talk. But that was not the end of Selkirk's adventures.

The Largo man rose to command in his rescuer — Woodes Rogers' — fleet, helped capture a Spanish treasure galley and returned to Fife. There was a girl here, and soon a house with children, but always the memory of his solitary years haunted him and he would wander the denes of Fife.

However attractive his wife, the sea was his mistress and she lured him back. It was inevitable, and so was his death when he found himself cruising the West Coast of Africa.

'Beware and take care of the Bight of Benin,
Where one comes out for forty goes in!'

Selkirk did not come out; the fever got him and he was tossed overboard. But as Crusoe, Selkirk lives on and his statue perpetuates a little of the reality that the book hides. Fittingly, there is a Largo hotel named after the book, equally fittingly it is beside the sea.

But Largo had another seaman, less famous yet perhaps more deserving than Selkirk. Andrew Wood was his name and he is known as Scotland's Nelson. Wood was a fighting seaman when the fifteenth century was closing, a friend of kings and enemy of pirates. With his two ship flotilla of *Yellow Caravel* and *Flower,* he held the Forth for James the Third until that monarch was murdered after Sauchieburn fight. Thereafter, Wood was pulled into the orbit of the fourth James, son of the slaughtered king.

Ambushed at Isle of May

A trader as well as a warrior, Wood was returning from Flanders when he was ambushed by three English ships. The English, under one Stephen Bull, had hidden in the lee of the Isle of May, used a captured fisherman as lookout and pounced on the Scots.

The fight was long and hard, spears and archers busy as the grappled ships spattered their light cannon. The sun sank on the tattered, weary crews.

Drifting northward, all five ships resumed the battle next morning and crowds lined the banks of the Tay to cheer. Wood needed no encouragement; his men were experts and Bull's ships were soon towed as prizes into Dundee.

For this and other endeavours Wood was awarded lands at Largo, in the shade of shapely Largo Law. His castle was here, with easy access to the sea, easier to the church. Using his English prisoners, Wood carved a canal from castle to chapel and was rowed in state by his old crewmen. It must have been quite a sight, the elderly admiral cruising down the canal while his men laboured loyally at the oars.

Largo Law dominates this section of the coast, but Norries Law, to the north, has a greater claim to fame. An iron age tumulus, it was plundered by a tinker in the early nineteenth century and a collection of Celtic silver was unearthed. Greedily, the tinker sold his finds, an unscrupulous silversmith melted down the artefacts and the treasure was lost. Later excavation found other pieces which are kept safe in an Edinburgh museum. Only a small story, but it leads to speculation; how many other hoards have been lost to thieves, and how many remain scattered and unknown round the shores of the Forth?

Anstruther — and a tale of the Spanish Armada

The good people of Anstruther must have held their breath in apprehension when the great galleon carved her way out of the North Sea and headed directly to them. There would have been consternation, hands reaching to grasp weapons or to hide precious possessions, men searching for their wives and mothers for their children. Troubled times had returned to Scotland.

It was 1588 and there was war. Spain, the colossus of Europe, had launched a tremendous armada against her heretic enemy, England. As usual, the Scots had become involved. Some co-religionists offered help to the Spaniards and rumours of secret meetings and quiet landings abounded. Queen Mary was not long in her grave and there was little love for her executioner cousin — but another war? Surely Scotland had suffered enough!

As the galley closed it became apparent that there was no

danger. Sea voyaging had taken bitter toll, cords and lines were in tatters and the crew looked weary, half starved.

News of the English victory in the Channel had spread, and here was proof; this was a survivor of a defeated fleet, not the vanguard of invasion. Tempers changed in Fife and sympathy replaced fear.

Into the harbour, anchor chain roaring and the tall ship swung, a pike to the minnows of the Anstruther fishing fleet. A pause, an exchange of civilities and the Spanish commander, Gomez de Medina, clambered ashore. He would look about him at the dull harbour, the high gabled Fife houses, the fishing clutter on the quay, and would feel at home; a seaman among men of the sea. There was no animosity to an impoverished mariner, no history of wrecking in Fife.

James Melville, the Anstruther minister, was among the "honest men" who met Medina at the Tolbooth — Anstruther's Town Hall. Medina was frank; the Armada had been defeated, more by weather than by warfare, and his section of the fleet had run aground at Fair Isle, between Shetland and Orkney. The crews had nearly starved. A small, impoverished island, Fair Isle had not enough food, if a surplus of kind humanity.

Now Medina asked the help of Anstruther, but could offer nothing in return. Asking nothing, Anstruther rose to the occasion. What they had, the fisherfolk gave freely. They fed the gaunt survivors, presented them with all the spare clothing in the village and helped them on their way back to Spain.

Medina was lucky; galleons wrecked on the west coast of Ireland had their crews massacred without pity.

On his way back, Medina put in at Calais, maybe for water, perhaps for information. Instead he found the crew of a fishing boat. The fishermen were under arrest, and they came from Fife, from Anstruther itself. Surely this was one of the most intriguing coincidences in history!

Medina proved he was a Spanish gentleman. Praising the good qualities of Scotland, he had the Anstruther men freed

and bought them a boat to return home in. Asking to be
remembered to the minister, Medina bade the Fife folk farewell
as they ploughed north. An example of international co-
operation which should be better known.

Biggest herring port

Fishing continued in Anstruther, and still does, if in nothing
like the volume that saw the town as the largest herring port in
Scotland during the 1930s. True to their fickle nature, the
herring fled the Forth as they had Loch Fyne; following the
shoals around the Scottish coast is an art. Also an art is
developing a museum, and Anstruther has one of the more
interesting in the country, dedicated, of course, to fishing. Even
the museum building has its attraction, for its site is doc-
umented back to 1318 — unusual for a piece of town
property.

Anstruther's other claim to fame is its lyrics. Maggie Lauder
was an Anstruther lass, and her name is bawled out in folk clubs
all over the country. On the other hand 'Anster Fair' has rather
slipped in the popularity stakes. And that is a pity, for this is a
fine, jocular piece of ribald libel which races along easily.

"Her lovely ladies, with their lips like rubies,
Her fiddleres, fuddlers, fools, bards, blockheads,
blackguards, boobies"

What a description, and nothing like the Anstruther of
today!

Why a stone at Crail Kirk helped Bruce at Bannockburn

If Cramond is incomparable, Crail is surely unique. A view of her harbour is carried on many glossy calendars, and rightly so. A handful of fishing and pleasure boats huddles in limpid water beside an olde-worlde harbour wall. Above them is a street of centuries old houses, gently rising to an unseen, tantalising destination. Crow gables step above pull-sash windows and a single lamp post stands central to light the way. This is correct; Crail had this atmosphere and has worked hard for it. This is probably the most attractive village in all the coast of Fife — although most others would hotly dispute that!

Before it was recorded as anything else, Crail was a fishing town. Back in the ninth century, when Pictland was more than a memory and manuscripts reported little more than never ceasing warfare, Crail had a thriving export business with the continent. She exported fish. Trading links last long in the East Neuk; the Low Countries still saw Fife boats in the eighteenth century and possibly after that. Salted fish put Crail on the map and salted fish kept it there. Forth caught herrings were sent to the king in the bitter years of the English wars, and Crail Capons — haddocks hung to dry in the sun — brought prosperity to the village at the tip of the Neuk.

There is still fishing in this part of Fife — hopefully there always will be — but the focus has moved westward to Pittenweem. The boats are there now, with all the character and the bustle, but Crail was first.

In between the fishing, Crail men had a notion to be warriors. When Robert Bruce was gathering his forces for the arranged encounter at Bannockburn, the men of Crail strung their bows and readied their gear. Being of Pictish stock, they did things with style; they asked guidance from the Lord and used a stone outside His church to sharpen their arrows.

This stone can still be seen, scraped outside the Church of St Mary's. This is a fascinating building, founded in 1175 and still with some original stonework. It seems that stones play a large part in the culture of Crail, for as well as the sharpening stone there are two, beautifully decorated, from the Pictish period and one massive blue-grey boulder with a story attached.

It was in the olden days when Auld Nick was in the habit of flaring up from Hades to visit the surface, and he decided to look at Fife. Half blinded by the brimstone, he miscalculated his route and emerged on the Isle of May. He was so enraged by his mistake that he took his bad temper out on St Mary's Church, clearly seen from the island. Lifting a stone, he hurled it clear over the sea and now it remains embedded at the church gate as a reminder of the spleen of Lucifer.

But not only Auld Nick ranted at Crail; his deadly enemy John Knox did likewise and possibly for no better reason. Knox visited St Mary's when in his heyday and delivered a splendid sermon of bombast and damnation. Perhaps he wanted to outdo the devil, or maybe it was Crail's centuries old privilege of Sunday trading which annoyed him so much. That had been granted by Bruce as far back as 1310, so possibly the Crail bowmen had sound commercial reasons for supporting him at Bannockburn.

From Crail there is an excellent walk eastwards to Fife Ness, the very tip of the Kingdom. A rocky, white breakered coast with a one-time Royal Naval airbase to the left. From here stringbagged Swordfish flew to defy the most military power in the world, and slightly further on a turfed wall of earth was meant to control earlier Teutonic aggression. How effectively is shown by Constantine's Cave, where King Constantine ended his reign at the point of a Viking sword.

Once there was a village here, the Royal Burgh of Fife Ness. Nothing remains but a solitary, spray tainted cottage beside the golf course. Bunkers and greens hide the spot where Mary of Guise stepped ashore to be greeted by the Laird of Balcomie. Mary was travelling to meet the fifth King James; in time Mary would become as big a menace to Scotland as any female in history. Perhaps it is fitting she should share her Crail connection with John Knox and the Devil, for all are long ago and extremities of religion fail to mix with the open beaches of the East Neuk.

Scotland's first lighthouse and a witch called Eppie

Seen from the coast, the island of May is a slight white smear on the horizon. It appears insignificant, even ethereal, a ghost island. Yet May is solid, a mile long island of cliffs and rock, of tufted grass and wheeling, calling birds. Names on this island are evocative: North and South Ness (a Norse word meaning promontory); Maiden hair; Altarstanes; the Pillow. Then there are the remains, the Priory and the lighthouse, and somewhere in the southern half, under the grass will be the few shattered remnants of a once thriving village. Not only west coast islands once held a population.

Today, birds rule this island while the lighthouse beams its warning to radar guided shipping, but it was not always so peaceful. As usual there was a saint or two. The mythical saint Ethaeman, the legendary Adrian — unless they were one and the same — and enter the Vikings. One Christian hermit against a shipload of ruthless young thugs; exit the age of saints. Adrian was placed in a stone coffin, which floated to the shores of Fife. Implausible, but perhaps saints' powers increased after their death.

In the thirteenth century the Norse menace had ended and the English were not properly started on their aggressions, so May was reasonably safe again. A chapel was set up on the island, dedicated to the martyred Adrian, and soon after this a Royal Rabbit preserve was announced. It seems a long way out for anybody to want to go and poach rabbits, but maybe Fife fishermen had a taste for them.

Kings seem to have had a fondness for May; both the third and fourth Jameses cruised out to visit the chapel, or maybe to check on their rabbit stock, and much later an exiled eighth James was to anchor offshore before an abortive attempt to recapture his lost kingdom. Between them were Andrew Wood of Largo's sea battle and the first lighthouse in Scotland.

It was the beginning of the seventeenth century and the Forth was busy with shipping. Unfortunately not all the ships reached their intended destinations; there are said to be some four thousand wrecks between the Forth and the Tay. It became obvious that something had to be done. There had been lighthouses before, of course, but never in Scotland, and to place one on May seemed a good idea.

Originally a great metal basket filled with coal, the light was a direct descendant of the invasion warning beacons of mediaeval times. Once a string of them stretched from the Border northward.

Known as the Beacon, the lighthouse still stands, hiding its grisly history. As it was being constructed, the architect was drowned in one of the sudden Forth squalls and an unfortunate female of Anstruther, Eppie Laing, was accused of creating the storm by witchcraft. Naturally she was found guilty and burned at the stake.

In the next century there was another disaster when the lighthousekeeper and his family were found suffocated by coal fumes. Their deaths had caused the destruction of a ship, to add to the toll. Lighthousekeeping was a dangerous occupation in the Scottish isles!

After an attempted invasion in 1708 which saw a French fleet outmanoeuvred off May by the Royal Navy, an English seaman said this:

"While we were on board we had continual Distruction in ye foretop; ye Pox above board; ye pleague between decks; hell in ye forecastle, and ye Devil att ye helm."

And that was the victorious fleet — who would be a sailor on a night like that?

Flight o' the Jacobites

Seven years later another threat appeared.   The Old Pretender, James Stuart, was on the loose and white-cockaded armies rose from the Highlands to fight for him. One force of Jacobites, under Mackintosh of Borlum, marched into Fife and proclaimed James the Eighth in the villages of the East Neuk. Hanoverian men of war patrolled the Forth to ensure the Jacobites could penetrate no further south, but Borlum had the answer.

Sending a diversionary company to Burntisland to draw off the navy, he gathered all the boats he could and thrust out for the opposite shore. One thousand men crossed in the first wave, one thousand still to go, but the second trip was not so successful. The Royal Navy appeared, scattering the flotilla of small craft. The majority of Jacobites landed at North Berwick, one boat was captured and others scurried to May Island for safety.

For days Lord Strathmore and his men languished on May, Highland and Lowland together as the October winds whipped the sea and the fifteen fishing families who lived on the island wondered.   Highland argued with Lowland as frustration mounted and it was not until the Navy was blown out to sea that

Strathmore's party could return to their headquarters in Perth.

May had not seen its last encounter, but no more armies landed. The island remains aloof from both Fife and Lothian, still a place apart.